ROAMING THE WILD

ROAMING THE WILD

Portraits of Wyoming

Grover Ratliff

Sastrugi Press

San Diego • Jackson Hole

Sastrugi Press / Published by arrangement with the author

Sastrugi Press: 2907 Iris Avenue, San Diego, CA 92173, United States
www.sastrugipress.com

Roaming the Wild: Portraits of Wyoming

The author has made every effort to accurately recreate conversations, events, and locales from his memories of them. To maintain anonymity, some names and details such as places of residence, physical characteristics, and occupations have been changed. All photos and text contained herein are copyrighted by the author and registered with the United States Copyright office. As such, they may not be reproduced, copied, distributed, reprinted, published, displayed or broadcast without the written permission from the author and/or publisher. The publisher does not have any control over and does not assume any responsibility for author or third-party websites or their content.

Library of Congress Control Number: 2014948691
Ratliff, Grover
Roaming the Wild - 1st U.S. ed.
Summary: Grover Ratliff has photographed northwest Wyoming for over a decade and his work represents the epitome of life in and around Grand Teton National Park and Yellowstone National Park.
ISBN-13: 978-0-9960206-4-0
ISBN-10: 0-9960206-4-0

Printed in the United States of America

10 9 8 7 6 5 4 3 2 1

Dedication

To my dear and wonderful Mom and Dad, Laura Olivia and Grover Cleveland Sr.

To my first love and wife, Dorothy, for nearly 58 wonderful years before I lost her.

To my four wonderful kids, three grand kids and two great grand kids.

To my now dear love and wife, Bettye, who helped put my life back together and made my life whole again.

To all my present and past great friends and family.

To all that have made me who and what I am.

And, to my dear Lord for 90 years of blessings.

LOVE

Introduction

Another photo book? Why?

GOOD QUESTION!

There are thousands of photo books in or on every book rack, book store, photo gallery, super market and every souvenir shop in Jackson Hole already. They are all produced by a number of renowned professional photographers in this area. Prices range from $9.00 to $100.00 table top books, so why another one?

I have a gallery of my own in the Lexington Hotel in Jackson Hole. The Lexington decided they would like to decorate with photographic prints and I am the lucky friend they chose. I get to meet folks nearly every day from all over the world and get to share what I love so much about living here. In 2012, at the insistence of my friends and hotel guests, I produced a DVD of a number of my photos and have found that there really was a market for my images.

Recently a book publisher came into my gallery, looked at my work, and suggested that we should produce a book. So now, you know WHY!

My first interest in photography was sparked by a high school friend who had a camera. He got to take photographs of the girls, sports, and everything else for the school newspaper. Then, watching him in the darkroom develop his film, I became enthralled. But I did not have a camera–I was just envious. However, I was 15 at the time and had a paper route. There was a newspaper delivery contest one month and the prize was a camera. I sold more subscriptions on my route than anybody else, won the sales contest, and secured my first camera. It was a Kodak Brownie that used 620 film that produced a 2 1/4" x 3 1/4" image. It was a treasure. I was trapped and now I have always had a camera for the last 75 years. I now have a powerful device to capture thousands of "magic moments" in my life as I have puttered along.

Landscapes and wild flowers caught my eye in Texas hill country in the early 1940s. Soon, I moved on to Kodachrome color slides and I was hooked for life.

I have witnessed the evolution from black and white film, to color slides, to color film to the digital age. What a interesting journey it has been. As interesting as it has been, I sure don't miss the darkroom time, the smell of the chemicals, the red light, or the waiting for an image to show up in the chemical tray. We have come a long way, baby.

There is never a day when I am out that I don't see images, in any direction, that I feel I need to shoot. With our equipment of today I shoot all types of images, from honey bees, rocks, flowers, landscapes, wildlife, skies and everything in between.

I can't imagine anyone not having a computer and a camera to go with it. They don't know what they are missing. Out of 180,000 images I have shot in the last twelve years, once in awhile I get a keeper but always hope the next shot will be the best.

Grover Ratliff

Photography in the Tetons

The Moulton barn is always a challenging yet wonderful area to try to take your all time best shot. However, when the temperature is below zero and I am out before day light and the wind is blowing, I can't help but wonder if this was a good idea. Waiting at the Moulton barn with 13 other camera nuts, a pesky cloud that I had been watching and hoping would be in the right spot instead blotted out the whole sky. There was no sunrise image that day.

On another occasion, I was following a midsize bull moose along the bank of a small creek. He didn't seem to be aware of me as I moved closer. That shows how smart I was. He turned and charged toward me. Of course, as old as I was, I don't run but hurried as fast as I could for ten yards. That was the end of my escape route. I hooked my toe on the sagebrush and fell down on my face, holding my camera and long lens over my head to keep from smashing it. When I looked back, the moose was standing there laughing at me. And to add salt to my wounded pride, I lost my cell phone and never found it. I bet the moose was wondering what the ringing in the sage was?

Sometimes, happy accidents happen with a wonderful result. In 2004, I was walking toward the Menor Store and noted some stacked fire wood behind it. I thought the stack of wood would make an interesting image with the mountains in the distance. I walked around the store and immediately a magic picture jumped in my face. There was an old window with a fantastic reflection of the Grand Teton in beautiful fall colors. It is one of my favorite images of all time, So, happy accidents always make up for the bad days. There are no bad days, some are only better than others.

One of my scary moments happened as I was walking along Pacific Creek road in the berry and bear season. I was on the edge of the road with my left shoulder brushing the bushes. Grizzly 610 stepped out in front of me and was just as startled as I was but not as spooked as me. We were about eight feet apart. After a few moments, she turned and walked away from me about thirty feet, turned around and began growling at me. After that, she decided she had the upper hand and walked on up the road, leaving me speechless. It was a special experience but once was enough.

Another berry season, I was on Signal Mountain among some huckleberries bending over as I was picking and eating them faster than I could pick. I happened to look up as a black bear was coming toward me doing the same thing. I gave up and let him have the rest.

I never know when something special will pop up. Along Moose-Wilson road one day, my friend Jim was with me and noticed a sandhill crane's nest on the edge of a pond. He has younger eye balls and I would never have seen it myself. I was lucky enough to watch her a couple of weeks as she tended her nest and kept a watchful eye on her two eggs. A cow moose approached too close to the nest and I saw her peck the moose in the butt and run it out of the water. I checked every morning for two weeks hoping to catch the little ones hatch. It happened after my morning visit, on July 4, and before my evening check. Sometimes you miss them.

Another time Jim and I were driving in our own vehicles. We saw a huge herd of bison on the right side of the road. They were walking toward us as if they might cross in front of us. We both stopped on the side of the road with our vehicles eight feet apart. I leaned back on the front of my car and Jim was leaning on the side of his car protecting him from the bison. We waited for them to walk past. All at once they began to run for some reason. They parted and ran both behind and in front of our cars just as we hoped. But one big bull decided he didn't want to run around two cars. He ran full speed between me and Jim's car. I could almost feel him rub my knees as he charged by. I'm not sure but I think I heard Jim say something like, "Holy scat, did you see how close he came to you?" I replied, "Yeah, for sure! I was there."

The Gros Ventre campground is a perfect area to explore for animals. However, in the fall after the campground closes is the best time. Back when I could still walk, my great amigo, Jim Laybourn, and I, hiked in around the closed gate and had the whole area to ourselves. We found two large bull moose snoozing in the snow about thirty feet from us. There were some small shallow bushes that we knelt down behind and began shooting. The moose had not noticed us at all. All at once, the bulls noticed a cow and calf running past us, on our left. They jumped up to chase the cow and ran straight toward us on our knees. They were almost on top of us when they saw us and ran past. Whew! Another fun day in the campground.

In the summer of 2013, my walking and standing became extremely difficult for me. I had to resort to riding a small three wheel scooter to keep moving. Bear jams are always a big problem and they make parking difficult, as people stand shoulder to shoulder along the road. But now I find my scooter provides a better view than anybody. Moose-Wilson road is always a interesting area and one day there was a bear jam day and I must have been the last guy there. On my scooter, I rolled past dozens of cars. I poked my camera between people and since I am so short sitting down, I got away with it.

The black bear was working his way downstream. It was warm this day and I knew there was a pond down the way. I thought the bear would move down and take a swim in the cool water. My scooter took me to the pond before nearly everyone and I waited. Patience paid off and I was able to take some shots of him swimming, scratching and then shaking the water off. I enjoy my scooter because I can mount my camera on a monopod on the scooter and I have a three wheel tripod with a seat.

A sunroof is a safe and advantageous way to shoot bear pictures. My wife, Bettye, is smarter than me. She won't exit the car if we are in bear habitat. So the hole in top of the car is her chosen position and it has worked out for her. She now takes better pictures than me. One day I decided to try it. I'm a rather big guy at 190 pounds but managed to stand up through the hole. However, Bettye had to climb up there with me. With both of us up there, there were four too many elbows and two too many cameras to function at all. It didn't work out. I thought it best for me to leave her in her space. Wriggling back into the car wasn't easy, so I won't do that again.

Three sub-adult grizzly siblings hung around together in the Togwotee pass area for several weeks in the fall of 2013. We frequently found them and always managed to capture good images along the road from the window of my car. However, I have more fun when I can be on my scooter and enjoy being on their level. One of the bears started toward me and most folks began yelling to jump back in your car. As I can't walk well, it wasn't quick or easy to do, let alone hurry. The bear wasn't looking for trouble, nor was I.

The only advice I have is: venture out early and stay out late. It is wonderful how often you will catch a happy accident. Every day is another chance for a real keeper of an image.

The Swainson's hawk migrates to Argentina for the winter, one of the longest migrations of any American raptor. These gorgeous buteos, a large hawk with a broad wing and short tail, are frequently seen sitting on fence posts and drain pipes around Jackson. These birds are highly social and are found in groups outside of mating season.

The American Kestrel is the smallest member of the falcon family. This is the only shot I have ever taken of this beautiful hunter.

Great grey owls are the largest of the owl family. I think they have the most interesting face of all. Their wingspan can be as much as 60 inches and body length to 33 inches. They can be found in heavily forested areas and some times on fence rails along Spring Gulch Road, Moose-Wilson Road, and Murie Road. These are all prime places to watch for them.

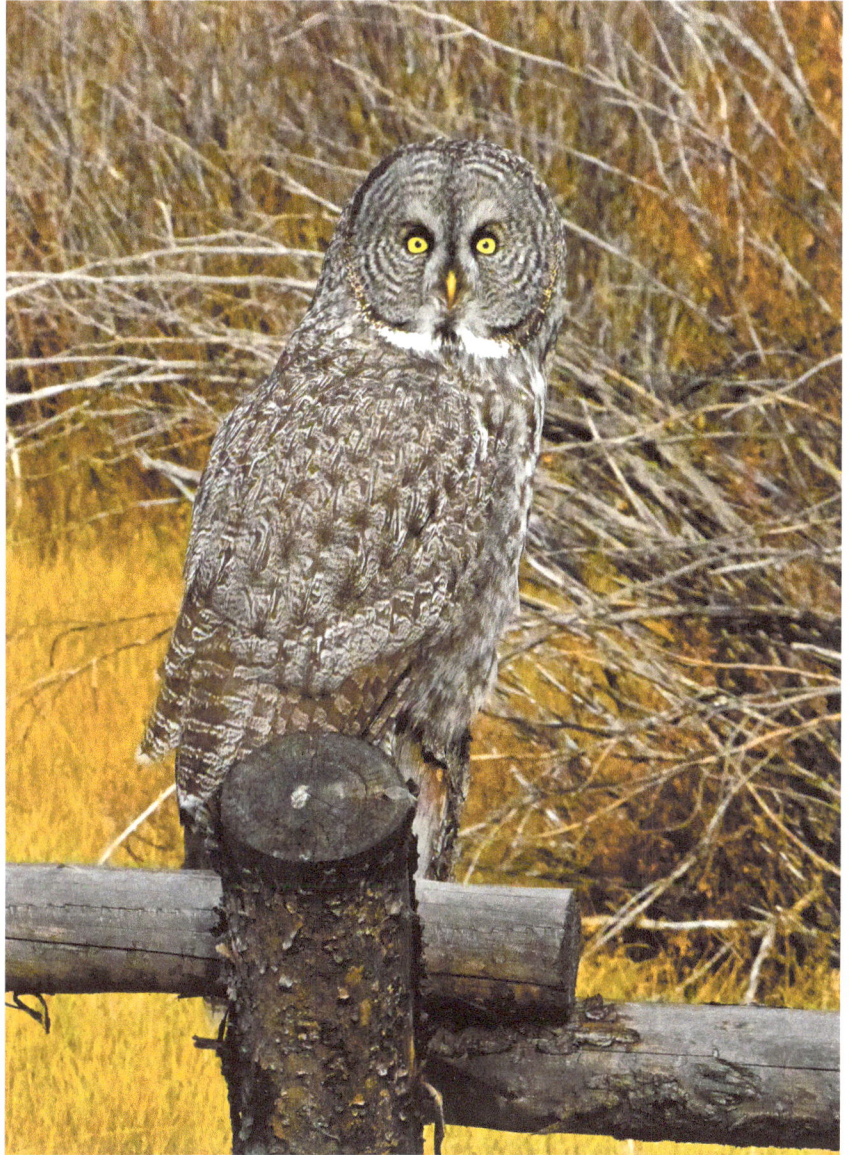

"Don't know why it was named golden eye."

This Barrow's Goldeneye was swimming on Flat Creek behind the Dairy Queen in north Jackson. This section of the creek is an excellent place to see water fowl after having an ice cream treat.

7

This is not a baby bird being fed. These tree swallows are mating. The female is only about half as large as the male. Their backs are iridescent and they nest in cavities or bird houses. They can be found flying around and under the bridge over Flat Creek in north Jackson.

(Facing page) Mountain goat's hooves are hard on the outer edge but have a soft pad in the middle which enables them to hang on to the smallest point of rock. Though not indigenous to the area, mountain goats adapted well to their surroundings after being introduced in the 1940s and 1950s. They can be regularly seen in the Snake River Canyon near Alpine in the winter.

MOUNTAIN GOAT ON ROCK

GROVER RATLIFF

Back when I could still walk, I was ambling along the Gros Ventre River one savagely cold morning and there were these beautifully God arranged rocks that the snow had melted off of. I could not pass the chance up of making an image out of these. This is my favorite rock image of all my 75 years taking rock pictures.

Lower Yellowstone Falls

My favorite of the two waterfalls of Yellowstone is 308 feet tall. It is best viewed from Artist's Point for the most spectacular perspective. Sometimes you can see a rainbow in the mist.

SANDHILL CRANE

The sandhill crane is a large member of the crane family and has a wing span up to five feet. Their natural color is dove gray but in the Teton area they are a warm tan color. Our local bird expert tells us that they preen themselves with mud for better camouflage. I watched this bird nesting for two weeks but still missed seeing the two eggs hatch. Just my luck.

The Chapel of the Transfiguration is the most beautiful little log church that I have ever seen. It's located north of the entrance into Teton Park and is quite old but not quite as old as me. I am 90 and its only 89. It's open all the time to visit and enjoy. It is truly a spiritual experience with a view through the chapel window with the cross pointing to the Grand Teton. The pews are made from split logs. There are two beautiful stained glass windows–one for winter and one for summer. The artist has bordered the winter picture with snow flakes all different as they are supposed to be. You need to see it when you visit Grand Teton National Park - it is a special place.

The road toward Cody is one of my favorite byways. This image is six photographs stitched together to create this wide angle view. The lighting was perfect.

This nearly white coyote wandered alongside the road. The coloration is quite unusual and he didn't spook when we stopped. Perhaps he was too young to be afraid. His eyes were a striking gold color and he has been the most beautiful one I have ever seen.

GREAT HORNED OWL AND CHICK

"This took quite a while."

A bull moose eating fresh greens along the Gros Ventre River. Moose grow their imposing antlers every year, starting out covered in velvet. Later in the season, the velvet falls or is ground off, leaving the famously bony protrusions.

"Biggest litter I have ever seen."

"I'm embarrassed to tell where this location was. It was along Snow King Boulevard right in Jackson."

A vixen, or female fox, had a litter of five one season. This little one, licking his chops, was the most aggressive of all. When mom would return from looking for something to feed them, he seemed always to be the first to eat whatever she brought. She was skinny as a rail and looked like she never ate anything. This one kit always seemed to be the most curious.

17

A TENDER MOMENT

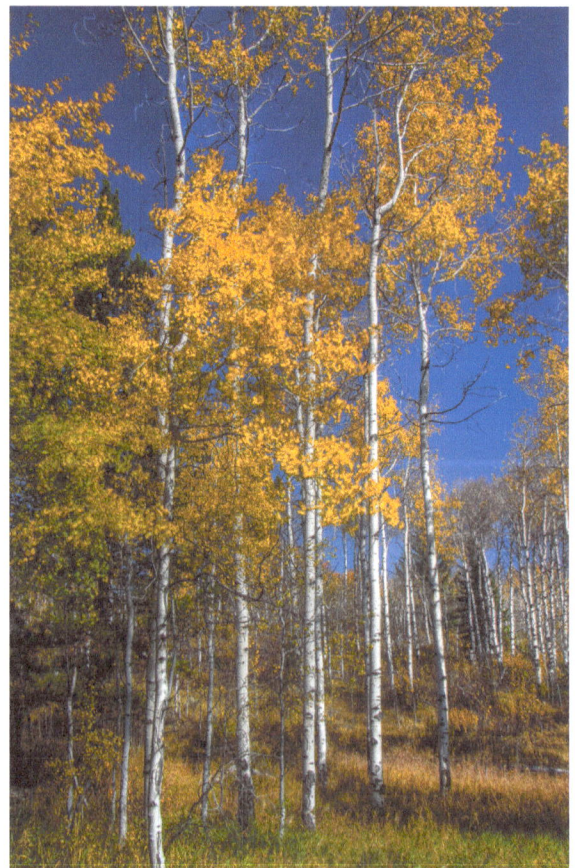

This is my favorite view of the Grand Teton: through the Chapel of the Transfiguration window. This picture was shot in September 2006. Sadly, most of the aspen trees to the right of the cross have died. Everyone should take this picture.

"I never tire of taking a look."

One has to be ready for anything while living in Jackson. There can be the chance to hunt, kayak or snowmobile. Sometimes all three can happen on the same day.

This was a harsh, cold day in the Hoback River Canyon. It seemed as if the magpie was attempting to warm his feet as he flew back three times to perch.

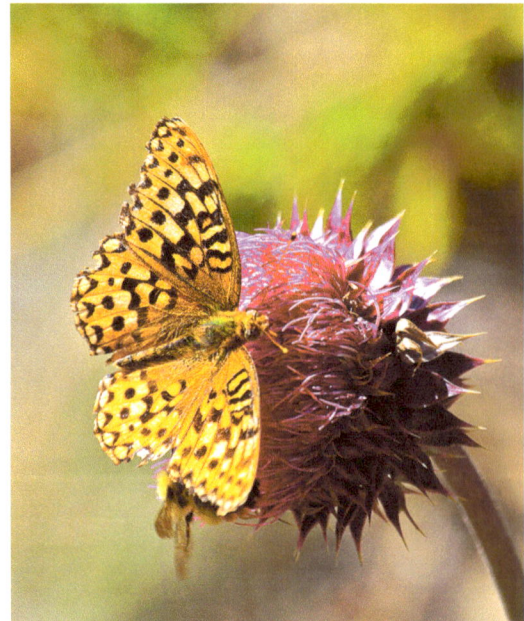

This view of the distant mountains always intrigues me. It is in the Buffalo Valley area at the Heart Six Ranch which is always a tasty place to catch a bite to eat.

This is the only one snowshoe hare I have ever seen and been able to take a picture of in my life. Their tracks are much more frequently seen than the actual animal. In a summer coat, he looks like he forgot to take his winter socks off.

Snowshoe Hare

I had been watching goats in Snake River Canyon from my favorite spot. While shooting, I noticed this billy grazing by himself when he jerked his head around, checking something behind him. Perhaps he spotted a girlfriend.

Moose are seen eating twigs and small trees year-round. Native Americans call them twig eaters.

"They like to keep their teeth clean, too."

23

"Wish I could have done this when I was young. WOW!"

(Facing page) A male dusky grouse changes his eyebrow color from yellow to red when he is courting a female.

This pair developed a full blown relationship. Initially, the ewe would not acknowledge him even being there. Disgusted and disappointed, he laid down while she continued grazing but he kept his eye on her. Several minutes later, another ram showed up and rushed over to her. The first ram jumped up and butted the interloper in the side and ran him off. Shortly after, the ewe and first ram were mating.

"Don't ever give up."

25

HARMONY

This spot is always interesting. A post and rail fence casts picturesque shadows along the river with the Tetons in the distance.

"I named this ram in front Scarface and took his picture for three years. He was easily recognizable."

Three grizzly siblings in the Togwotee Pass area, 50 miles north of Jackson.

I can never pass a chance for another photo of The Chapel of the Transfiguration in the fall.

A mule deer enjoying the morning sun after a cold night.

The Chapel of the Transfiguration

Many times, I find bulls like this in or near the Gros Ventre camp ground.

"The Gros Ventre is a good spot to get close-up shots from your window."

Near the north entrance to Yellowstone National Park in Gardiner, Montana. It was an extremely hot day and the animals were really suffering. Pronghorn are usually skittish and it is rare to see this calm of a photograph.

"Just don't fall on ice in the road and crush a bone in your spine like I did. I don't recommend it."

So many folks see a coyote and think it's a wolf, or wish it was. They are only about one third the size of a wolf. In Texas and Arizona, they are pretty ratty looking. But in the Tetons, they are beautiful.

This little red wagon rig always catches my eye each time I see it. It is at the gate to the Gros Ventre River Ranch. If there is a perfect ranch, this one is it. From a curve in the road you have a splendid view of the distant Tetons.

Traveling north of Jackson, on Highway 89, near Flat Creek, I was lucky enough to take this early morning shot of a swan at sunrise at the right angle. It was a priceless golden moment in time.

These beautiful animals are seen frequently in both Grand Teton and Yellowstone National Parks. As winter settles into the region, they migrate into the Jackson Elk Refuge area and in 2013 they numbered more than 8,000. Taking a horse drawn sleigh ride on the refuge allows many close up shots. Bald eagles are always seen on sleigh rides, too. Dress warmly because sometimes it is brutally cold. The Native American name for elk is wapiti which means white butt.

I was driving east on a curve on Antelope Flats Road on a frosty cold morning. As I passed through the curve, this most splendid sunrise I have ever seen jumped through my windshield. Most of the time, sunrise and sunsets last a few or several minutes. You might shoot several shots but not this one. Instantly, a small cloud began to nibble at the scene and, bam, it was gone. I only caught two shots. Always arrive at your spot before and stay until after.

I caught this handsome little black bear cub on the scenic Moose-Wilson Road, eating berries in the fall. This is a favorite road for you to see bears, moose, deer, beaver, elk, owls and other birds at almost any time. Drive slowly, as you might miss something.

(Above) He is the most perfect big-horn sheep I have ever seen. They congregate along the National Elk Refuge Road in the winter. This particular image was taken near Gardiner, Montana.

Anytime you can catch any wildlife with mountains in the background, take a picture, even though its a long way to the mountain. The image gains more depth and is much more interesting.

This cottonwood is one of my favorite trees. I take this picture every fall with Mount Moran in the distance. This is the last remains of a old homestead on Cattleman's Bridge Road. The road is a magnificent place to see bear, elk, deer, bald eagle, osprey, moose, beaver, pelicans, swans, geese and river otters.

I had never been so close before. In my excitement, I had a terrible time taking decent shots of this magnificent animal. It landed only 20 feet from me.

Golden eagles are a large bird, with a body length up to 28 inches and a wingspan up to 92 inches. Being much larger than the bald eagle, they are the tough hombre in the neighborhood.

GOLDEN EAGLE

River otters are more fun to watch than anything else as they play and cavort together. In the winter, Cattleman's Bridge Road is a magnificent place to watch them as they go under the frozen Snake River to catch a fish and come up on the ice. Frequently a bald eagle is watching from the top of a dead tree nearby and tries to steal the fish.

RIVER OTTERS, JACKSON LAKE DAM

45

GROVER RATLIFF

MOUNTAIN BLUEBIRD (FEMALE)

I found this little guy in January on Moose-Wilson Road late one evening near dusk. He was peeling and eating the bark off of the hawthorn bush. It was a treat, as he remained at this spot for four days and I took many photographs of him. Maybe he was born late in the year or lost his mom–he was found a week later frozen to death. He was only about as big as a large hairy football. He was the smallest porcupine I have ever seen.

Here's a photographic secret for you: on the back of the Menor Store, look at the first window you see. The Grand Teton is reflected in the glass and makes for a memorable image. Don't tell anybody else about this, though. There are a number of old wagons and relics from the era that are quite interesting also. When the ferry is operating, the crossing is now free. You can even eat at Dornan's and then ride over to the store and back.

Schwabacher's Landing is the greatest spot in Grand Teton National Park to take fantastic Teton reflections at sunrise. Come early to stake a place for your tripod. On a busy morning, there will be photographers lined up elbow to elbow.

STRENGTH

BEARS, BERRIES AND BUSHES

(Above) Berry season is the unbeatable time for seeing bears every year around Jackson. What looks like a pig is actually a grizzly peeking through the bushes.

"It was great fun to watch."

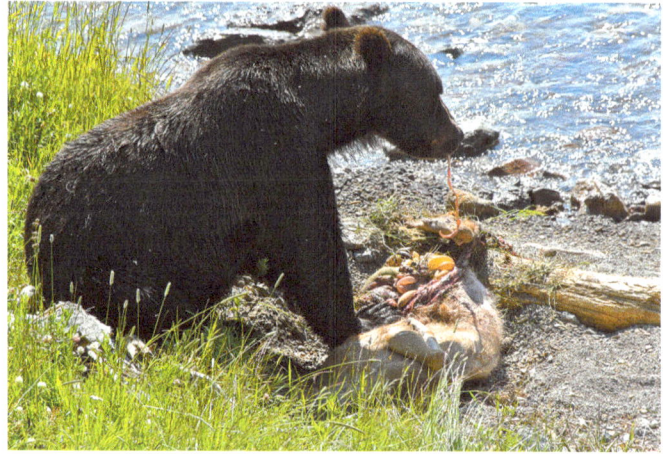

There was a big grizzly down on the shore of Yellowstone Lake feeding on a mule deer carcass and a cub was watching with envy. The cub would move closer, first on all four legs and then stood up for a better look. The big bear didn't pay any attention to him until finally, he turned his head to look up the hill at the cub. His glance made the cub run up the hill like his tail was on fire. It was eat, sleep, swim and then do it again all afternoon.

After all these years, I finally noticed bighorn tongues are blue.

On a late October morning, quite crisp and frosty. These bull moose tolerate each other but are only waiting for the rut.

In the winter, foxes have a unique hunting strategy. They stalk what appears to be open snow but are in fact listening for the sound of rodents under the surface. When they find their quarry, they leap up into the air and then dive face first into the snow to catch their meals.

Red foxes are beautiful, highly social, and true to their name - intelligent. This little one was squinting into the sunny day.

While in the Snake River Canyon, I had my best day ever: there were 53 mountain goats close enough to photograph for a half day.

(Facing page) Rough-legged hawks breed in the Arctic tundra but they are found in the Jackson area in winter. They pose nicely for photographers on fence posts north of town along the highway near the elk refuge. They are fascinating to watch while they are hunting.

(Right) This was the homestead of Thomas and Lucille Moulton, settled in the early 1900s on Mormon row. A half mile north is a barn of the homestead of John and Bartha Moulton, settled in the same era. These two iconic barns are the most photographed barns in the world, with the Tetons in the distance. Needless to say, these are a favorite spot for photographers. Even on a zero degree morning there will always be a group of camera nuts, like me, waiting for sunrise. But it is always worth it.

GROVER RATLIFF

MILLER HOUSE, ELK REFUGE

The National Elk Refuge was established in 1912. The first superintendent was Robert Miller and this house served as his residence. I took this photo on a bright December morning and it sure wasn't my fault that it turned out so nicely. The lighting was perfect and that made the picture look very much like a painting.

56

WISDOM

With such an interesting face, the great grey owl is my favorite owl. Even with their massive wing span, they make only a subtle whoosh sound as they fly over or near me. There must be a nest between Murie Center Road and Moose-Wilson Road because they are frequently seen in this area. Its always exciting to catch one on a buck and rail fence for a real picturesque shot.

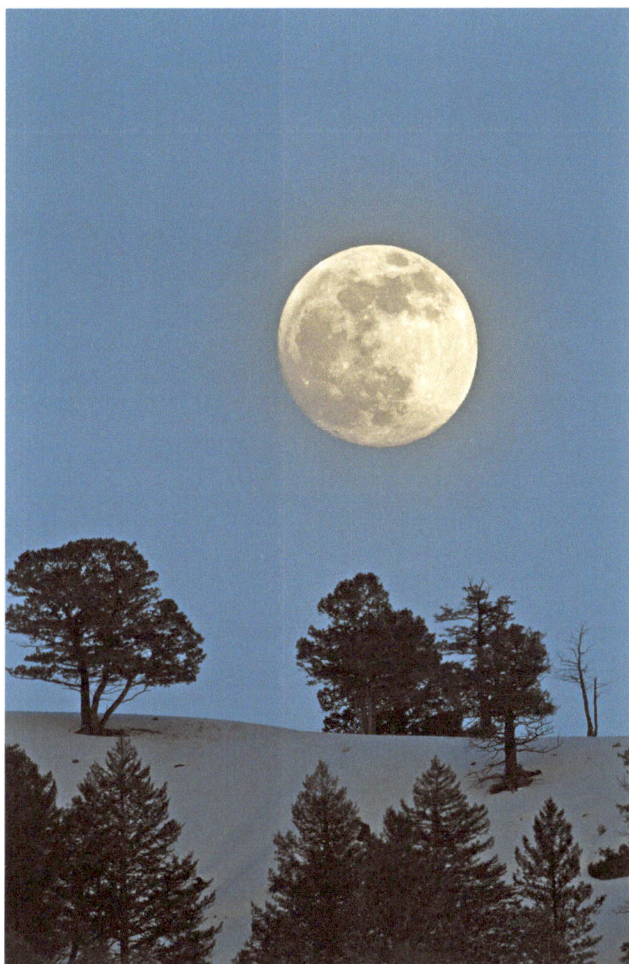

A clear cold winter night in Yellowstone presented me with my best moon shot ever. I happened to have a long lens with me this night, enabling me to make the moon appear that much larger.

57

When I see bison with snow on their face, I always have to stop and shoot it again. The way they put their face on the ground into the snow and sweep there heads to clear the powder sure looks like a hard way to make a living.

Old wagon relics are on the Gros Ventre Road in Kelly. I am amazed to think how often I have taken pictures of this junk pile at any time of the year. Having the Tetons in the distance makes anything look special to me.

This young moose calf was as startled as I was when I walked into him chewing on the willow leaves. This was on Cattleman's Bridge Road and is always a perfect place to find compelling photographs.

Great horned owl chicks in the heart of the cottonwood tree along the Gros Ventre River.

This bald eagle was perched in an old dead cottonwood tree about 250 yards north of Antelope Flats Road. Of course I didn't have any lens that would reach that far. I watched him with binoculars for a short time and decided that I could zoom in on him with my feet. I started walking slowly toward him, stopping for awhile and then walking some more. I finally came close enough to catch this image before he reacted. It was the first bald eagle picture I had ever taken, so I felt rather proud.

I found this ruffed grouse as I was driving slowly near Two Ocean Lake. He was on the ground and when I disturbed him, he flew 10 or 15 feet. I kept easing along and he finally grew disgusted with me and he flew up on a limb. I never did take a decent shot of him. Oh well–maybe another day.

BUCK AND RAIL FENCES

"No room at the end."

When early settlers came to the area, they found plentiful lodge pole pine trees to build their cabins and fences, though they learned that the pine fence posts rotted in the rocky ground which made digging post holes difficult. Building cross bucks and then laying a top rail made from lodgepole pine

trees was easier. This design made it possible to build a quick fence for corrals, etc. The first time I saw a buck and rail fence I was intrigued as they always made such interesting shadows. However, it looks as if the men putting up this fence ran out of cross bucks and resorted to using overly long top rails, creating the sagging fence.

This small three room log cabin, 100 yards from the Chapel of the Transfiguration, sits on the bank of the Snake River. Bill Menor built it in 1892 and set up a ferry service to shuttle customers across the river. It has what I would guess was the first auto flushing out house on the edge of a river bank. The kitchen and bedroom are both furnished as they would have been when it was built. Ginger bread cookies are freshly baked in an old wood stove every morning – arrive early if you want one. The front room is now a gift shop full of mementos and curios. The store even sells huckleberry soda pop.

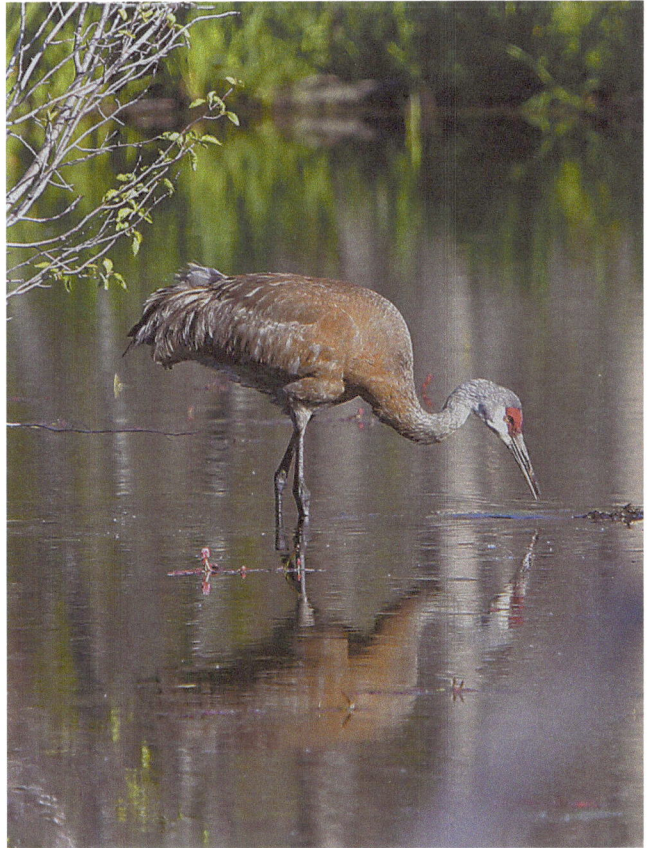

GROVER RATLIFF

"The location is famous for early morning sunrise shots. Come early and don't sleep in if you want to have the best chance at a wonderful image."

HORSE COWBOY SHADOW

This is a lucky shot at the old Moulton barn on Mormon row. Often, bison, pronghorns and song birds can be seen along the road and around these famous barns.

(Facing page) A couple of cowboys were at the Moulton barn one morning when I was there. It is one of my favorite images.

OXBOW BEND

About the author

Our little house was on a gravel road at 1441 East Jefferson Street. We lived at the end of the city streetcar line and one half block west of the Cotton Belt rail road track. That was always a fun place to play in the mud along the track. We hunted for crawdads in the bar ditch with string and a piece of bacon. When my neighborhood buddy and I had a penny, we could hardly wait for the next train to come and mash our pennies on the rail.

My school was a mile west of our house and I walked with a sack lunch every day. It was usually a bacon and egg sandwich with a piece of fruit. I still enjoy them to this day.

I always passed a big red chow dog on the way to school and he never paid any attention to me as I walked by. But one day, while returning home, he ran at me and nearly scared me to death. His chain jerked him to a halt and saved my skin. From then on, I thought it was entertaining to tease him and watch him get jerked to a stop. Then one day, the chain broke loose and he chased me all the way to our front door. I never tried that again.

My dad worked for the Rock Island Rail Road as a fireman. He shoveled coal to feed the boiler on the steam engine at that time. As

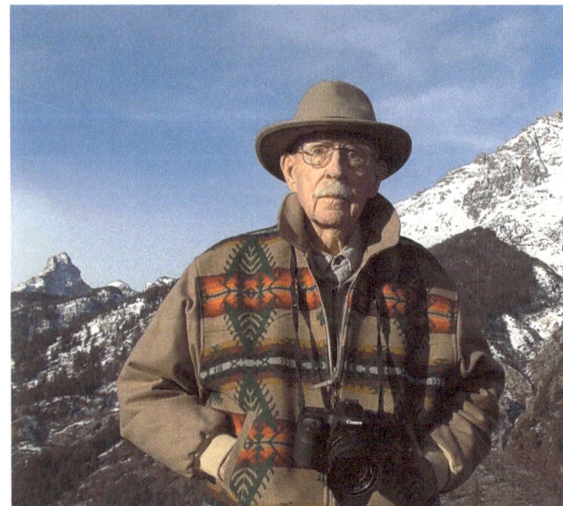

My first signed photograph

a kid, I thought that was a pretty neat job. But now, I don't know how he did it. In the financial disaster of 1933, Rock Island laid him off. Shortly afterward, he was diagnosed as having tuberculosis and was sent to a sanitarium in Carlsbad, Texas. It was thought he contracted it from his army service in World War I.

They sold our house and mom and I move to San Angelo, 16 miles southeast of Carlsbad. This allowed her to drive us in our 1927 model Chevy to visit dad every week. Being nine yrs old, I didn't realize how dire the situation was. Raw milk was 3 cents a quart and I had plenty to drink. I could walk to town on Saturday with a dime and see a movie. On the way home, I passed by the fire station. The firemen would let me climb upstairs and slide down the brass pole. I enjoyed every one of those days.

After a couple of years, dad was released from the hospital and we returned to Fort Worth. Somehow, he bought a little grocery store and we lived in the back of the store with a #2 washtub for our bathtub. I delivered

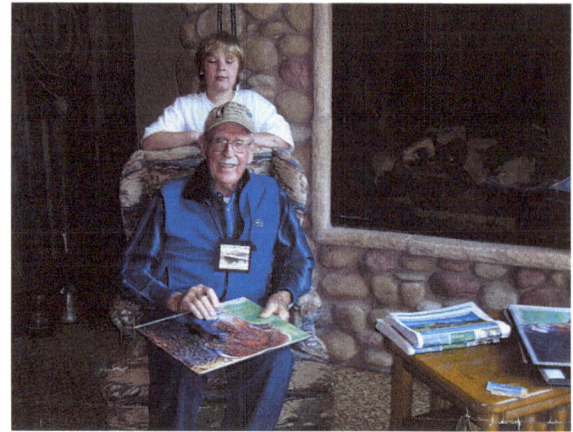

groceries on my used and rebuilt bike. It had 26" wheels on a 28" frame. It looked awkward and had bad tires. I used a tube of "never leak" to patch the flats.

As the financial crisis eased, dad regained his job on the rail-road and I felt we were on easy street again. Of course, I wasn't the guy shoveling the coal. I had the usual kid jobs: mowing grass, delivering papers, sacking groceries, and stacking beer bottles at the Totem Store (it's now a 7-11 store). During this period, I found my girlfriend and high school sweetheart on my paper route. We graduated from high school together in 1940.

After three years in college, I quit to join the army as so many of my buddies had already done. However, I received the shock of my life when I was declared unfit for the army. I was 4F. This scared me nearly to death as I thought I must be near dead already if the army would not take me during a war. Here I am, still alive, at 90 years old. I likely wouldn't have survived if the army had taken me.

I and my sweetheart, Dorothy, then both immediately applied for a job in the engineering department of Consolidated Vultee Aircraft Company (Convair) in Fort Worth. It was known as the bomber plant. They built B-24, B-32, and B-36 bombers during the war. Dorothy was hired as an artist and illustrator and did detailed pen and ink drawings for the pilot manuals. I was hired as a draftsman. Dorothy and I married in 1944.

Dorothy's first job was to detail a pilot's relief tube. Her boss was an older artist that she had known previously in art circles in Fort Worth. He placed the device on her desk and told her to draw it and write the copy for how to use it. She didn't know what it was let alone how to use it. It was great fun for those around her desk to watch her squirm and be embarrassed. Being in the engineering group, I became a liaison to the plant's mile-long assembly area. I am still amazed at what that plant was able to do. I learned a great deal and enjoyed the experience. Dorothy and I both left Consolidated in 1946.

I then went to work for the Texas Highway Department until 1952 on a drawing board and in the field. While working a second job, I still wasn't doing very well but did gain useful experience. After some time, I quit my job and was hired by a Dallas company as a sales engineer. It gave me a the cheapest two door Ford available and put me on the road with west Texas as my territory. My car did not have a heater or radio but I thought I was in heaven. From then on, it was mostly a good climb to a better way to make a living for which I am eternally grateful. From that start as a peddler, I worked up over the years to more fun and success than I would have ever dreamed possible. My last job ran from 1967 until 1996, when I retired at age 72.

In 1948 my wife, Dorothy, and I had a nutty idea – we wanted to see Alaska. We took off for Alaska in a four cylinder 1946 model Willys Knight Jeep station wagon. This turned out to be a 10,000 mile 6 week camping adventure. It was called the ALCAN Highway but it was just a road, believe me. We had a Coleman lantern and two burner stove. En route through Wyoming was our first time to see the Teton area. It turned out to be our favorite campground and still is. In later years, we finally got to come back on vacations. We traveled, ran and played together until I lost her in 2002 after nearly 58 years of a superb marriage. I came to Jackson Hole to try to get over my loss. It was our favorite place and I have been living here the last 12 years.

I have met another wonderful lady, Bettye. She and I will be married 10 years, January 1, 2015. She has morphed into a camera nut, too. With my cameras, I have shot nearly 180,000 images. Believe me, not all are keepers but I keep trying anyway. I can no longer walk but still enjoy shooting from my car window and my 3 wheel tripod with a seat. Nothing can be better for a good "bear jam" shot. I am still trying to get a keeper picture once in awhile.

Hope you enjoy the book.

Grover

MY TRAVELS TO ALASKA

1948

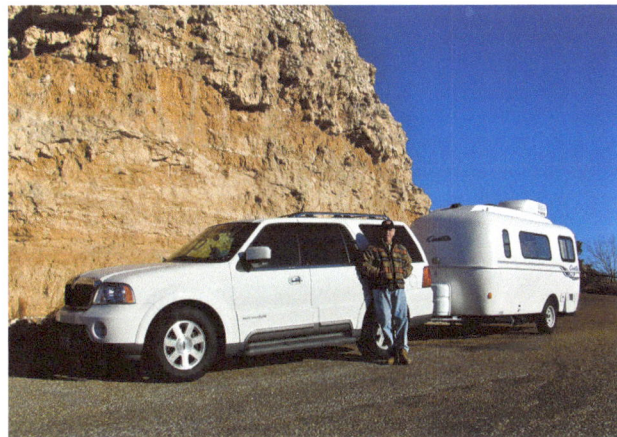

2003

Fort Washakie cemetery

An unusual grave yard north of town. Every grave is decorated in a very special way with some memento of the departed. This pair of boots tells a story without words, the end of the trail. It may be marked with a beautiful beaded belt buckle or a child's toy. A large statue of Sacajawea is dominant in the area.

In the summer of 2013, my walking became so difficult, I had to resort to a cane and a scooter. It now serves as my transportation and three wheel tripod with a seat. What a deal!

68

DATE: January 28, 2014
TIME: 4:13 AM
LOCATION: Jackson Hole, WY
LAT: 43.5ºN LON: 110.8º W
EDGE OF MY BED

Lamenting third pit stop for the night. Kinda like Dr Pepper at 10, 2 & 4. Both knees moaning and back is trying to decide which is worse, stay in bed or get up. From somewhere a voice said, "Howdy, a good morning to you."

What's good about it, everything hurts and nuthin works? Everything else either leaks or squeaks.

The voice said, "I am so sorry to hear that. Has it always been this bad for you?"

"Oh no!" I had never had to spend a night in a hospital till I was 82 for carotid surgery to remove a big chunk. The doctor said that I was in line for a certain stroke had it not been removed. That was too close for comfort.

Then in October 2010, a heart problem became serious, forcing me to have a quadruple bypass. Again, I feel that God and the fantastic doctors at Intermountain Medical Center in Salt Lake City saved my butt again.

The voice said, "Have you ever heard of three score and ten and do you know what that meant?"

Oh yes, the bible says that is the allotted time for man, 70 years.

The voice asked, "How old are you now?"

89, I'll be 90 in February, the 24th. Why do you ask?

"Well, your standard warranty ended 20 years ago, have you thought about that? You must have received the super double extended GOLD warranty."

Well, yes, I have thought about it a lot. I have made up a word for myself, "BLUCKY". Means blessed and lucky, mostly blessed.

"How has the rest of the parts of your life been?"

WONDERFUL! I had a beautiful wife, Dorothy, for nearly 58 years, four great kids, three grandkids and two great grandkids. I found another beautiful and wonderful lady, Bettye, to marry me and we now have been married nine years this January 1, 2014. I think she still likes me, too.

After I lost Dorothy, my friends in Jackson Hole invited me to come to Wyoming.

My dear and wonderful friends, Diana and Tim Waycott and Helen and Max Kudar took me in and adopted me into their family and I have been here ever since.

I have always had a camera since I was 15. And now Bettye and I get to enjoy this heaven on earth, here in the Tetons, trying for our next hopefully good photo.

Not bad for an old guy, is it?

Not bad at all.

What were we talking about awhile ago?

I'm not sure. I forgot.

Thank you for waking me up.

Grover

ATTITUDE

A bear jam and the author on his scooter.

Grover Cleveland Ratliff, Jr., born Sunday February 24, 1924 in Fort Worth, Texas.

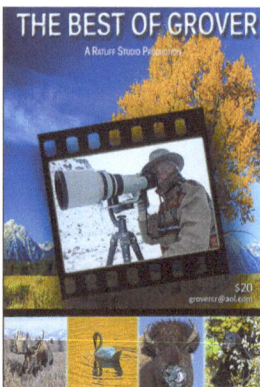

A companion DVD, *The Best of Grover*, is available for purchase through the author:
grovercr@aol.com
and at the **Lexington at Jackson Hole Hotel & Suites** in Jackson, Wyoming.

www.ingramcontent.com/pod-product-compliance
Lightning Source LLC
Chambersburg PA
CBHW041543260326
41914CB00015B/1531